THE FIRST BOOK OF FOOTBALL

THE ► FIRST BOOK ► OF FOOTBALL

JOHN MADDEN

Crown Publishers, Inc., New York

Photo Credits:

Arthur Anderson/NFL Photos, 33, 96; John Cordes/Focus on Sports, 63; Scott Cunningham/NFL Photos, 42; Focus on Sports, 9, 46, 71, 74, 77, 94; Jonathan Hayt/Focus on Sports, 20; Tak Makita/NFL Photos, 39; John McDonough/Focus on Sports, 67; Michael Ponzini/Focus on Sports, 68, 84; Chuck Solomon/Focus on Sports, 32; Rick Stewart/NFL Photos, 23; Jerry Wachter/Focus on Sports, 54.

Published by Crown Publishers, Inc., a Random House Company, 225 Park Avenue South, New York, New York 10003.
CROWN is a trademark of Crown Publishers, Inc.
Manufactured in the United States of America
Originally published by Crown Publishers in different form in 1988.
Library of Congress Cataloging-in-Publication Data

Madden, John
  The first book of football.
  Summary: Football and television superstar John Madden explains the fundamentals of football, including comments on what makes football great and ways to watch a game.
    1. Football—United States—Juvenile literature.
[1. Football] I. Title.
GV950.7.M24 1988   796.332'0973   87-37981

ISBN 0-517-56981-7 (trade)
ISBN 0-517-58593-6 (pbk.)

10 9 8 7 6 5 4 3 2 1

First paperback edition, August 1991

Contents

PART 1

Throw, Catch, Chase, and Kick

The Game Is Yours

Football is the greatest game going. It's exciting, it's fast-paced, it's unpredictable. And you can be part of it.

Anyone can play football. If you're big and maybe not so quick, you can be a lineman. If you're small and can run pretty fast, you can be a receiver, running back, or defensive back. If you like to throw, play quarterback. If you like to kick, you can be a punter of kicker.

There is a position for everybody. Every skill you need can be learned just by playing. As a matter of fact, that's probably what you should be doing right now. If it's still light outside, and not raining or snowing, why don't you put this book down, grab a ball, and go play. This book can wait until after dinner or a rainy day.

How do you play? Any way you want! Get some guys together, choose up sides, then kick off. Now you're playing football.

How many guys do you need? Three against three, four against four, eleven against eleven—it really doesn't matter. If there's an odd number of guys—say, five—you can play two against two and have a permanent quarterback, or you can substitute. Whatever you want.

The game is yours, and the only thing that really matters is having fun.

But, hey! Don't get the idea I think football is only a terrific sport for players. Fans have twenty-two guys on the field in a pro football game. That's twenty-two different things to watch. You don't have to keep your eyes on the quarterback. You can watch any position on the field and find excitement everywhere.

The very best thing, though, about being a fan is that you never know who's going to win. If you did, there would be no reason for cheerleaders to jump around and bands to play and all that television hoopla. There would be no reason to play the game. You can think your team is going to win, but there's no way to know for sure.

Will there be a fumble? Who will pick it up? Will there be an injury? Is there going to be an interception? Who's going to block a kick or miss an extra point? I don't know. You don't know. Nobody knows!

Even the pros don't know what will happen. A pro doesn't know how he's going to do. He hopes that he'll do his best, but he's nervous as heck—to the point of being scared.

Also, just like the pros, fans don't know who will win the individual, man-to-man battles throughout a game. Battles are won and lost in pro football on every play. And those contests add up to a team's victory or defeat. A pro hates to get blocked, or miss a block, or have a ball intercepted against him.

He hates to lose a battle, but he doesn't hate his opponent. That's something some people don't understand.

Hey, it sounds like a car crash every time the ball is snapped. But all those guys are friends off the field. Hit a guy, knock him down, help him up. Hating to lose but not hating the guy who beats you is what professional competition is all about.

For all those reasons, football is the best game there is.

When I played it was always fun, when I coached it was fun, and now that I'm a broadcaster, it's still fun.

I hope I can help you enjoy football as much as I do. That's why I wrote this book.

2

Football on Madden's Lot: Field Goals Were Never Big

All sports involve the same basic skills: hand-eye coordination, balance, concentration, positioning your body. But team sports can teach you an important skill for life: how to get along with people.

As part of a team, you always have to be thinking about your teammates. You can't just do your own thing. That's a term I always hated: "do your own thing." People don't get many chances to run around "doing their own thing." Mostly you have to do the best job you can within a group, whether it's school, society, or a team.

Individual sports can help you be a great athlete. They can teach you how to do your best. But if you only play individual sports, you're missing out on the friendships a team sport can give you.

When you're young, there's really no need to choose between sports to play. The best athletes are the ones who are good at everything. You should play basketball, football, soccer, stick-

Chapter 2
Football on
Madden's Lot:
Field Goals
Were
Never Big

ball, tennis, baseball, anything you can. Actually, I've always thought that your favorite sport should be whatever's in season.

If you only want to play football, and it's March, there won't be anyone to play with. Everyone will be playing baseball and basketball. If you want to play baseball in November, it's hard to get up a game.

I know because I was the kid who got the guys together.

I grew up near San Francisco, in Daly City, California. There was a small empty lot next to our house that everyone called Madden's Lot. I thought the place belonged to me. I found out that it didn't when somebody started building a house there. But until then, that's where my friends and I had games. And since it was my lot, I had to figure out how football was played.

So I went to Kezar Stadium, where the 49ers and the University of San Francisco played football, and just looked at things: where they put the yard markers, the boundaries, and how many points they got for what. Then I came back and we did it ourselves.

We'd play all kinds of football on the lot—touch, tackle, sometimes just short-yardage games. Put the ball near the goal line and see if you could score.

Nobody was telling us what to do because they didn't have organized youth leagues back then. There wasn't such a thing as Pop Warner, and I'm glad there wasn't.

Learning how to play football means learning how to organize, learning how to get together, learning how to lead. When everything's organized for you, the leadership is coming from adults. Leadership should be coming from you.

Learning how to play means running, jumping, throwing— those are natural skills. You develop those skills by playing and having fun. Adults may not mean to, but most often they keep the game from being fun. I thought that when I was a kid, and I think that today.

Playing a game with friends lets you play at your own level. You know best what you can do. You know better than some youth league football coach who's yelling at you. Your body tells you what you can do. You can make up your own games better than an adult can. And the experience can make you a better athlete.

Walter Payton, the greatest running back in history, never played organized football until his sophomore year in high school. His older brother, Eddie, was on the football team, and until Eddie graduated, Payton's mom wanted one of the kids home to help with the chores. So Walter was in the band.

You don't have to play football at all when you're young, yet you can still make it to the NFL. Playing tag is a lot like playing football. The great running back, as a kid, was never ''it'' playing tag. Walter Payton was never ''it.'' Who's going to tag him?

On the other hand, Joe Jacoby, the Washington Redskins' offensive tackle, was always ''it.'' So whether you're never ''it'' or always ''it,'' you still can become an All-Pro. How about that?

Chapter 2
Football on
Madden's Lot:
Field Goals
Were
Never Big

Former Chicago superstar Walter Payton—the greatest running back of all time.

How to get started

Until you have the proper equipment and the proper kind of supervision, touch football, not tackle, is the only game to play. Even guys in the NFL play touch football. Aside from some scrimmages, that's how the pros practice.

The team with the ball is the **offense** and they're trying to score. The team trying to stop them from scoring is the **defense**.

A play is called a **down**. The offense has four downs to score or to get a first down. If they don't score or make a first down (and they don't punt or go for a field goal), the ball goes to the team on defense.

In the pros, you get a first down by moving the ball ten yards. But you can change that in your game. A first down could be making it past midfield, or by making two or three complete passes, or whatever suits your situation.

The offense lines up just behind the ball. An imaginary line from the tip of the ball straight across the field is called a **line of scrimmage**. Neither team can cross it until the ball is snapped, and the quarterback can't pass if he runs beyond it.

You should have goal lines, the width of the boundaries, on both ends wherever you play. The offense moves the ball downfield toward the other team's goal line. When they make it across the goal line, into what's called the **end zone**, it's a **touchdown**, and that's worth six points.

If the offense gets caught behind their *own* goal line, that's called a **safety**—and the team on defense gets two points.

On fourth down, a kick through the goal posts, a **field goal**, is worth three points. After a touchdown, a kick through the goal posts is one point, an **extra point**.

Field goals were never big on Madden's Lot. Sometimes if some guy kicked the football up in the air, we'd say it was good.

When you start a game, flip a coin or something to see who kicks off. It's an advantage to get the ball, so you want to receive.

Any time a team scores, they kick off to the other team. The only exception is when the defense gets a safety, the offense

Chapter 2
Football on
Madden's Lot:
Field Goals
Were
Never Big

kicks off. That's why safeties are so valuable. You get two points, then you get the ball and a chance to score again.

When we played, we tried not to worry about penalties too much. When somebody did something wrong, we'd say, "Don't do that!" You're not allowed to hold on to another player; that's called **holding**. You're also not supposed to do something called **pass interference**, interfering with a player catching a pass. About the only penalty we had, though, was **offsides**. That's when somebody jumps past the line of scrimmage before the ball is snapped. "Hey, you were offsides," someone would say.

And that's really all you need. In fact, you probably don't even need all that.

When you watch football, it'll be played on a complicated level. But when you play a game with friends, it shouldn't be complicated. You don't want to complicate your game with rules. Rules aren't important. The more rules you have, the more you'll end up like a bunch of nerds, saying, "You can't do this because you were in the neutral zone, and you can't do that because it's illegal procedure." The more you worry about rules, the more the game will stop, and the less you'll play.

Don't spend a lot of time talking. Don't spend a lot of time with rules. Run, throw, catch, kick, and chase. That's football.

As for technique, the best coaches you could have are on television throughout a season. Watch great players do great things and copy them.

If you want to learn basketball, watch Larry Bird or Magic Johnson, and then go out and try to be them.

In football, if you want to be a running back, watch a great one. Watch a Barry Sanders or a Neal Anderson, see what they do, then do it yourself.

If you want to be a kicker, watch a Morten Andersen kick soccer-style, or a Tony Franklin kick barefoot. Watch the kicker on the sidelines, how he warms up. And then when the game's over, go outside and copy him.

There'll be technical stuff in a game that you can't copy. If you see that the defense is playing 3-4 and the outside linebacker is coming in from the weak side, where the offense has to shut him off with a tackle (don't worry if you don't know what all that means—I'll be explaining those pro terms later on), you really can't copy that kind of thing. But you *can* imitate the individual things.

Watch the guy you'd like to be. If you're tall, and you want to be a receiver, watch the moves of a Jerry Rice or a Sterling Sharp. If you're fast, there's Willie Gault, or other track-type receivers. And if you're not fast or tall, you can watch a Phil McConkey make the big play.

There will always be McConkey types in the NFL—players that everyone says are too slow, too short, too this, too that.

In Super Bowl XXI, Phil Simms passed to Mark Bravaro in the end zone. The ball went off Bravaro's shoulder . . . into the hands of Phil McConkey. Touchdown, Simms to McConkey. NFL computers must have blown their fuses.

But that wasn't some fluke. That was alertness. You'll never hear anybody called a superstar for alert play. But watching a player will show you that alert play wins games every time.

Chapter 2
Football on
Madden's Lot:
Field Goals
Were
Never Big

When you watch a guy throughout a game, you'll also see that running backs don't always run, receivers don't always go out for a pass, and linebackers don't always blitz.

Linebackers have to drop back and play against a quick and powerful tight end. Backs and receivers have to be able to block. They all have more than one job to do.

If you want to be a lineman, just watch those guys. Or a defensive back, or a fullback, or a quarterback. Watch how the quarterback drops back after the snap, how he looks for his receivers, how he throws. You're copying the best, and there's no better way to learn than that.

PART 2

The Pros
and
What
They Do

The Guys
with
Neat Lockers:
Offense

3

Guys who play offense usually have neat lockers. Offense is orderly. The offense has assignments. They know the play. They know when the center is going to snap the ball. They know who they have to block.

Offense is neat; it's organized. Every play is an organized attack. Running backs follow their blockers, who open up gaps in the defense. Receivers run pass patterns to beat the defensive coverage. Coaches design hundreds and hundreds of plays that are hundreds and hundreds of different ways to get the ball downfield.

There are really just a few terms you need to know to understand offense.

> **backfield**—back from the line of scrimmage
>
> **formation**—the way a team, on offense or defense, has lined up
>
> **strong side**—the side of the offensive line with the tight end
>
> **weak side**—the side of the offensive line without the tight end

A basic offensive formation with *strong side right* can look like this:

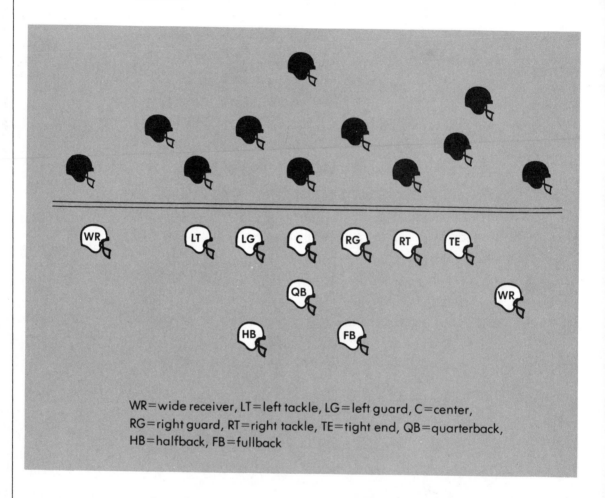

WR=wide receiver, LT=left tackle, LG=left guard, C=center,
RG=right guard, RT=right tackle, TE=tight end, QB=quarterback,
HB=halfback, FB=fullback

Now if this base was the only offensive formation, the game would be simpler than it is. But simple is easy to beat. Players change formation in football for two reasons. Certain formations are built for certain kinds of plays, and changing formation keeps the opposing team off balance and guessing about what's coming at them.

The snapper, pullers, and blockers: offensive linemen

The only players who *always* line up the same way are the five guys in the middle of the line.

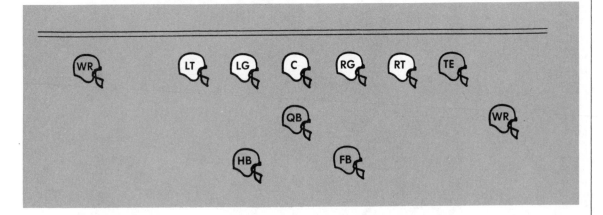

This five-man group is called the interior offensive line. In Washington, they call them the Hogs. No matter what you call them, this is where offense starts. They work together as a unit to block for the run in different combinations and to give pass protection for the quarterback.

Their fundamental job is to block the defense one-on-one. These guys have to have size, strength, and power.

The **center** is the snapper. He snaps the ball to the quarterback on the count, and the action starts. He's got to be big and quick to make that snap and then get both hands up to block.

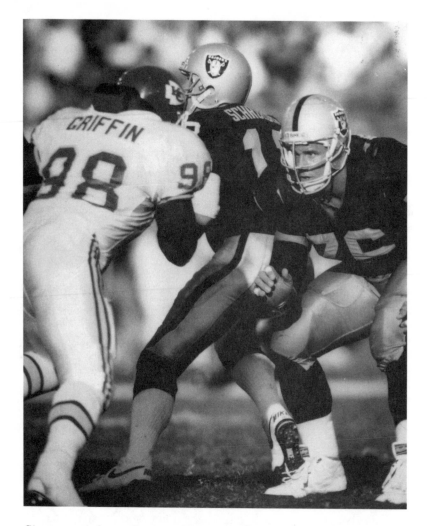

Size, strength, and power: Steve Wisniewski of the Raiders pre-pares to block for quarterback Jay Schroeder.

The **guards** move around to block more than anyone else. They pull (that means moving sideways instead of straight ahead) to lead a sweep, or they pull to take out a defensive lineman on a trap play.

The **tackles** are mostly straight-ahead, stationary blockers, so they can be bigger and slower than the guards.

Here's a look at three kinds of blocking. The T symbols stand
for the block.

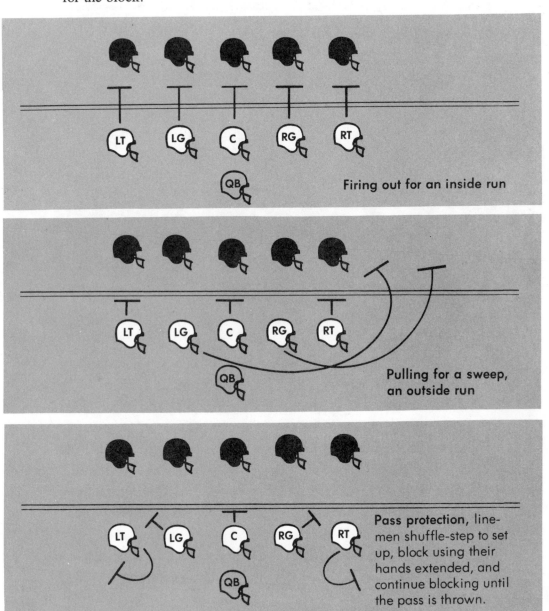

Firing out for an inside run

Pulling for a sweep,
an outside run

Pass protection, line-
men shuffle-step to set
up, block using their
hands extended, and
continue blocking until
the pass is thrown.

The passer, catchers, and runners: backs and receivers

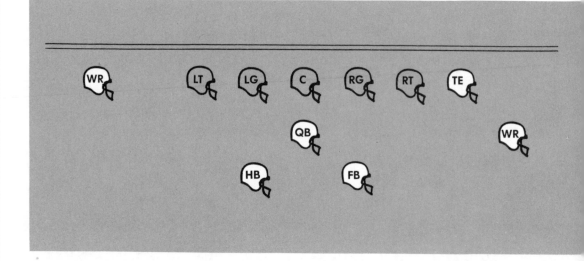

Pass receivers need an attitude. They need to believe that any time the ball is in the air, it belongs to them.

The **tight end** is part receiver and part offensive lineman. On a passing play he'll go out for a pass. On a running play, he blocks. He doesn't *help* block, as some would believe. He blocks.

Tight end is a very special position. Not many people have the combination of strength to block a big defensive player along with the agility to run a pattern and catch a pass.

Wide receivers are just that. They're pass catchers who line up wide. And you hope that they can block a little, too.

Tall guys have an advantage at wide receiver because the quarterback can see them better downfield. They also have a better chance of beating a shorter defensive back. But, tall or short, speed and quickness (along with the ability to catch the ball) are the important things for a wide receiver.

The wide receiver on the line of scrimmage is playing in a position known as **split end**. The wide receiver who has lined up back from the line is playing a **flanker** position. He often becomes the motion man.

San Francisco's All-Pro wide receiver Jerry Rice in the end zone, looking the ball right into his hands.

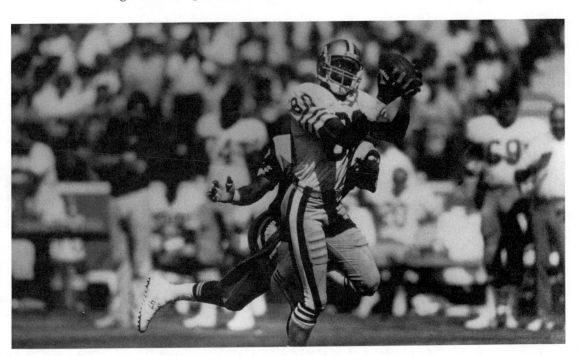

A man in motion is moving behind the line before the ball is snapped. He's giving the defense a big unknown: Where is he going?

There's another reason a wide receiver will line up at flanker. In football, some players are not legally allowed to catch a pass. Players at the very end of the line, and players (including the quarterback) at least a yard backfield, are eligible receivers— eligible to catch a pass. Everyone else is an **ineligible receiver**.

Look at the strong side right formation we showed. On the weak side, you've got a wide receiver at split end; he's eligible. The left tackle, left guard, and center aren't eligible because none of them is on the very end of line. Now, on the strong side, if the wide receiver at flanker moves up to the line, look what happens.

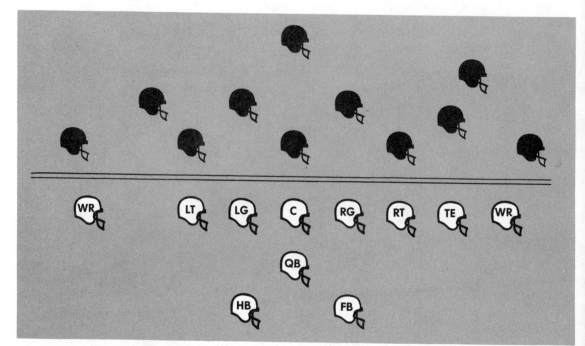

The tight end is no longer at the very end of the line. He's now ineligible for a pass. In this example, you've got five eligible receivers: the two wide receivers and the halfback, fullback, and quarterback.

Ineligible receivers are not allowed downfield on a passing play, but they are on a running play. This allows guards to go downfield on a sweep.

So now we have our eligible motion man receiver, our tight end, and our split end. But we're not done giving the defense things to worry about. Those defensive players are sharp. Let's throw more things at them.

Pass patterns give the defense another big unknown. Some common patterns are shown on the next page.

Okay, so you're an NFL receiver. You want to make the defensive back, the defensive player who is covering you, afraid of you. And that means making him think you're going deep. Going deep means "touchdown." You want to charge at the defensive back as if you're going deep every time. Then when you go out for a short pass, he's going to be off balance or out of position. We got him beat.

SHORT PATTERNS

A **slant** is used when the defensive back is playing away from the line. You charge out, take two or three steps, *bang!* go to the middle, way in front of the man covering you.

A **quick out** is the same kind of thing. Take a couple of steps, then cut to the sidelines.

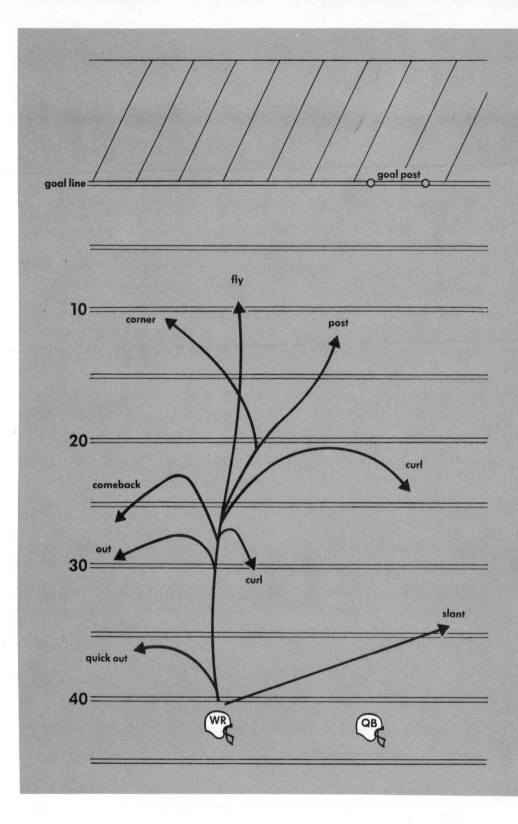

MIDDLE AND LONG PATTERNS

These patterns all start with the same kind of **stem**. A stem is a charge straight ahead (usually for eight to twelve yards) that will look the same for almost every pattern. You don't want the defense to know where you're going to go. They shouldn't be able to tell if you're going on a post, a fly, or any other pattern until it's too late for them to keep you covered.

The length of the stem, whether it's eight, ten, twelve, or fifteen yards, depends on a couple things. The first is the speed of the wide receiver. If you're a slow guy, your quarterback is going to get sacked by the time you've run for fifteen yards. If you're a fast guy and you run an eight-yard stem, that's too short, because the quarterback won't be ready to throw yet.

Another factor in the length of the stem is a very important thing about pass receiving: You're not just trying to catch a pass. You're there to get a first down or touchdown. When it's third down and ten yards to go, you don't run a nine-yard pattern. You've completed the pass, hey, but now it's fourth down and your team has to punt.

On an **out**, break toward the sidelines at an angle, coming back toward the line of scrimmage. Running straight gives the defensive back a better chance to get between you and the ball. Running at a slight angle can create a cushion between you and the defender.

The same idea is involved in a **curl**. You create a cushion by moving back toward the line of scrimmage. Moving toward the ball is against human nature, and it's a difficult way to make a catch. The easiest way to catch is to stand still and wait for it. But if you do that, the defense keeps moving and they're going to bat down the pass or intercept it.

On a **post**, you run the stem, break to the defensive back's inside shoulder as if you're going to curl or go in, get him turning the wrong way, then cut up the field toward the goal post.

On a **fly**, you give the defensive back a little stutter step, as if you're heading out or to the post, then you go straight upfield.

A **corner pattern** can be a very tough pass to complete. The quarterback has to be perfect on a very long throw. The receiver is just a few yards from the sideline, and in a straight corner pattern, the defensive back is with the receiver every step of the way.

The way to run a corner is to do the stem, head for the post for about five or six yards, then break back for the corner. Now you've given the quarterback more space to work with. He can throw the ball up, and you can run under it with room to spare.

All this talk about "breaking" may sound like a mysterious skill. It really isn't. When a receiver is running the stem, the defensive back is backpedaling. His shoulders are square and he can go in any direction the receiver does. Once he goes out of his backpedal and starts to run, the receiver is in control and can get past him.

On a corner pattern, for instance, when you break for the post, the defensive back has to break too and run with you. Now you can cut behind him, and the defensive back has to turn around to stay with you. While he's turning, you've got him beat. Touchdown, you.

Let's move on to **running backs**. One back will usually be a smaller guy who's a very nifty runner, and he's paired with a bigger guy who's a power runner and blocker.

The power back is the **fullback**. The **halfback** is the primary runner. He'll block and run short pass patterns, too. He'll also get **screen** passes, passes thrown to a receiver behind the line of scrimmage.

Running backs need to react quickly. They should explode through a hole the blocking has created, look for defenders from the front or either side, adjust to the defense, and go. They need to know when to cover the ball with both hands, and when to switch to one hand. You can run faster, and with more agility, when you're carrying the ball one-handed, but it's easier for the defense to strip the ball from you.

Here's an example of a running play. It's called a strong side lead play:

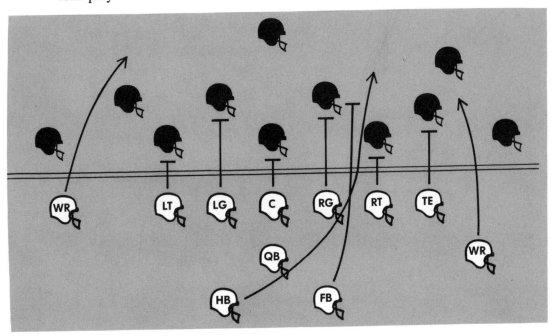

The fullback is not assigned a man to block. He's going to block anyone who shows. He leads through the tackle and guard, creating a hole with his blocking.

The halfback comes across the backfield, toward the inside foot of the tackle. He'll hit the hole, and head for the open field.

There are variations of this basic type of play. It can be run to the strong or weak side, with the halfback leading and the fullback carrying the ball. Throughout a game, you want to mix your ball carriers and blocking. Keeping the defense off balance is as important for a good running game as it is for the passing game. That's why running backs change formation, too.

At some point during a game, you'll see the running backs line up directly behind the quarterback. They form a straight line from the center like this:

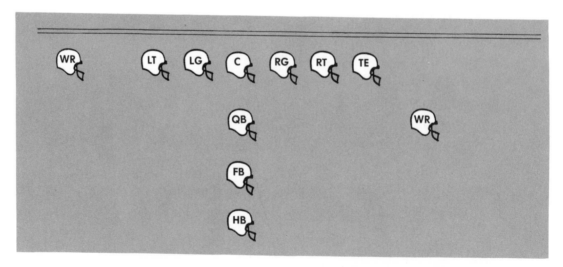

In this formation, the halfback is in a position known as **tailback**. It's called an "I" formation and it's used a lot for running plays.

The **quarterback** is the leader of the offense and he has to be very smart. He gets everything going. He passes to receivers, hands off or tosses to the backs. He's in the game to get the ball downfield.

A quarterback needs quick feet. He has to drop back from the line of scrimmage after the snap, away from the rush, and get set to pass. He has to judge when to stay within the pocket of pass protection, and when to move out.

He needs quickness in reading his receivers and releasing the ball. He has to see who's open and throw with accuracy.

Pass patterns aren't just things for receivers to run. They're also things for the quarterback to throw. He needs velocity and accuracy to throw long passes. He needs touch to throw shorter ones.

He needs quick hands on handoffs. The running back doesn't grab the ball, the quarterback hands it to him. He puts the ball in the runner's stomach, then gets out of the runner's way.

A quarterback needs every skill a person can have, including the ability to stay cool under tremendous pressure. I'll show you what I mean.

Kenny Stabler was one of my Raider quarterbacks. One year we were playing the Colts in a play-off game that turned out to be one of the longest games in NFL history.

A pro game is divided into four fifteen-minute quarters. At the end of the fourth quarter, the score was tied. We went into a fifth period, sudden death overtime—the first team to score wins. But nobody could score in the fifth period either.

The fans were going nuts. We started driving downfield, got to the Colts' 13. Stabler came over on a time-out.

I started talking about plays, waving my arms around. We ought to do this, we ought to do that. Stabler was facing me with his helmet tipped up, taking a drink.

"You know what, Coach?" he said.

"What, what, what?" I thought he had a play.

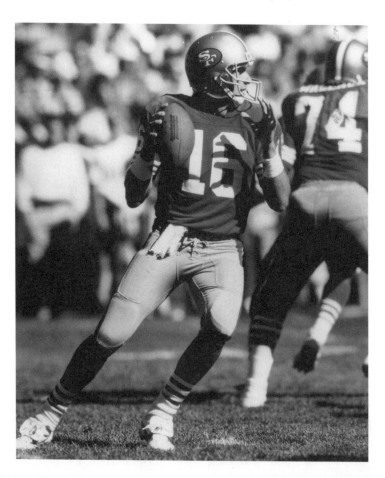

When the game was on the line in the fourth quarter, two of the best quarterbacks I ever saw were Joe Montana of the 49ers . . .

He looked at the stadium full of people and said, ''These fans sure are getting their money's worth today.''

Then he went in and hit our tight end, Dave Casper, for a touchdown pass that won the game.

That's staying cool. And that's offense.

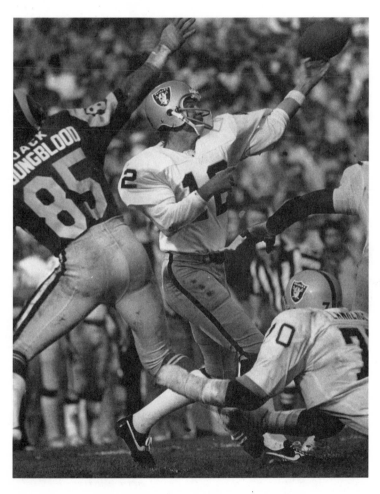

and my Raider quarterback, Kenny Stabler. Cool under pressure.

The Guys with Messy Lockers: Defense

Defense has one basic job: stop the other team's offense and get the ball back.

Almost everything the defense does is a reaction. When the offense runs, each defensive player has an assignment. If the offense passes, each player knows what to do. But the defense can only guess which it will be and where the play will go. They're stomping the ground, ready for anything.

It takes a special kind of guy to love playing defense. They have a certain look in their eyes. They chew their mouth guards. They're sloppy. Carefree. They react; they just go.

But they go within a system.

Here are some basic defensive terms that you'll be hearing:

the secondary—the defensive backfield (cornerbacks and safeties)

4-3 defense—four defensive linemen on the line of scrimmage and three linebackers away from the line

3-4 defense—three defensive linemen and four linebackers

short-yardage defense—as many as eight defensive players up on the line of scrimmage

long-yardage defense can include **nickel defense**—a fifth defense back replacing a linebacker; **dime defense**: a fifth and sixth defensive back replacing two linebackers; **quarter defense**: a fifth, sixth, and seventh defensive back replacing three linebackers

A standard 3-4 defense stacked up against a strong side right offense might look like this:

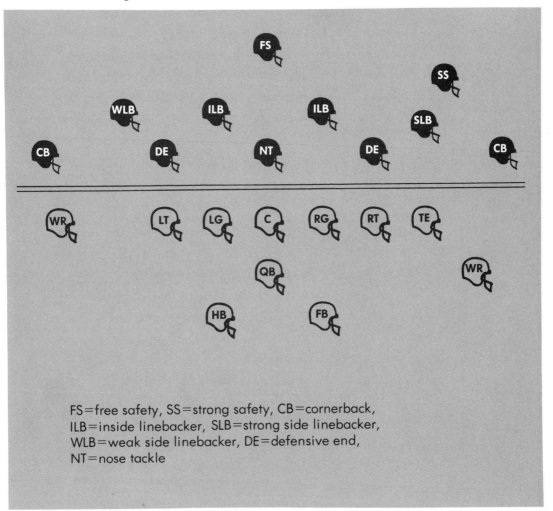

FS=free safety, SS=strong safety, CB=cornerback,
ILB=inside linebacker, SLB=strong side linebacker,
WLB=weak side linebacker, DE=defensive end,
NT=nose tackle

By the way, *short* and *long* in football generally refer to the distance from a first down, and they're really not precise terms. Third and short, for instance, means that it's third down and short yardage, say one or two yards, to go for a first down. Third and long means that it's third down and more than a couple yards to go for a first down.

> **zone defense**—defensive backs and linebackers are responsible for covering areas on the field
>
> **man-to-man defense**—defensive backs and linebackers are responsible for covering a specific pass receiver

All of these are ways that the defense tries to win the battle. There's a lot for the defense to beat: there's passing, running, and blocking. The defense tries to match, ideally overmatch, the offensive attack.

Hold the line and push it back: defensive linemen

The ends and tackles on the defensive line are usually bigger than the other defensive players. They don't run much. They all need very quick feet, long arms, and strong hands.

Defensive linemen work together as the offensive linemen do. A three-man line divides the line of scrimmage into thirds. They must be able to hold the line. They're in there to stop a run, and to rush the quarterback on a pass.

When a defensive lineman is playing right over the center, he's called the **nose tackle**.

The **ends** are usually the most effective pass rushers. They try to come around the offensive tackles and get the quarterback.

There's more to pass rushing than sacking the quarterback.

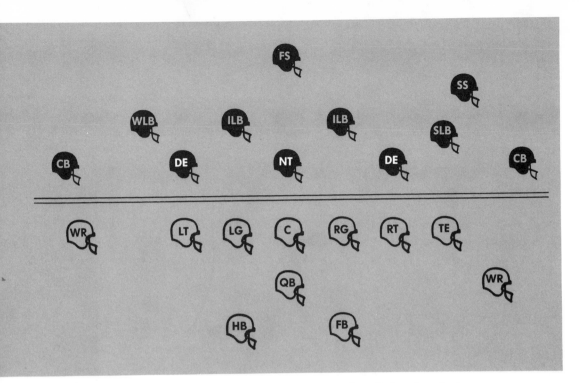

Effective pass rushing means getting your hands in the air to block the quarterback's vision. It can mean deflecting a pass and allowing your side to intercept.

Hand strength is very important for defensive linemen, particularly on a pass rush. They use their hands to grab, pull, and jerk an offensive lineman out of the way, and to beat a block.

All-around strength is important in defending against the run. A defensive lineman may be double-teamed by offensive blocking if the running back is coming his way.

Defensive linemen are usually a little taller than the offensive linemen, and not as heavy. They need to move quickly. They need to move the instant the ball is snapped. A defensive lineman who is a little late will have trouble. If the blocker gets to him before he moves—that's a battle he'll never win.

He moves on the snap and takes on the blocker using his hands. It's very important that the defensive lineman gets his hands on the blocker. That way when he sees where the ball is, he can throw the blocker and make the tackle.

The guys in the middle: linebackers

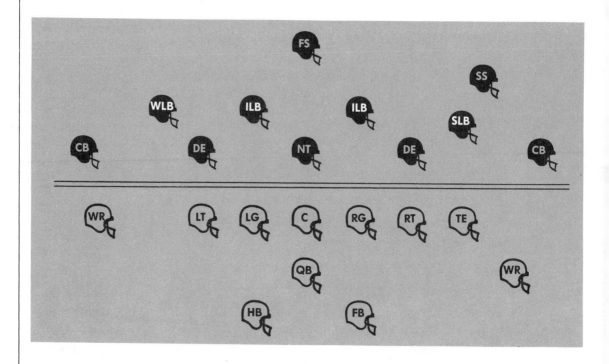

In life, there are three kinds of people: people who make things happen, people who watch things happen, and people who don't know what's happening. Linebackers make things happen.

Instinct is more important than size in a linebacker. When you have football instinct, you can play linebacker.

The dominant linebacker position used to be the middle linebacker, guys such as Sam Huff, Dick Butkus, and Willie Lanier. But today, with a 3-4 defense being so common, the dominant guy is the **weak side linebacker**. Lawrence Taylor, for example.

He'll rush the passer, and the offensive tackle has to shut him off by himself. On the weak side, there's no tight end to help double-team. And when you're blocking a live bullet like Taylor, you need all the help you can get.

What's wrong with this picture? Hey, somebody forgot to block 56! He is about to introduce himself to the man with the ball—"Hello, I'm Lawrence Taylor."

The **inside linebackers** don't rush as much unless the defense goes into some form of blitz. He's there (like the **strong side linebacker**) to stop plays—runs or short passes in the middle.

All linebackers need to be good tacklers. A solid tackle may be the difference between no gain and a big gain by the offense. When confronted with a block, they need a defensive lineman's technique to shed the blocker. A linebacker needs to know what the opposing team can, can't, will, and won't do from different formations. He needs to read the formation and react to the play.

Against the pass, there are two techniques a linebacker has to learn, the techniques of zone and man-to-man. If the coach has called for a zone defense, you simply cover an area of the field. Before the pass has been thrown, you don't follow a receiver out of your zone, because that opens your area for *another* receiver who won't be covered.

In man-to-man pass defense, you play against the back or receiver you've been assigned.

The secondary: defensive backs

The biggest responsibility of the secondary is to play against the pass, zone, or man-to-man. But they are also a back-up force against the run. Once a runner gets past the linemen and linebackers, the only defense left is the secondary.

The **cornerbacks** are defensive versions of wide receivers. A cornerback covers them all the time. He has to be a good cover person. If he isn't, he'll get beat for six points every time the offense passes deep.

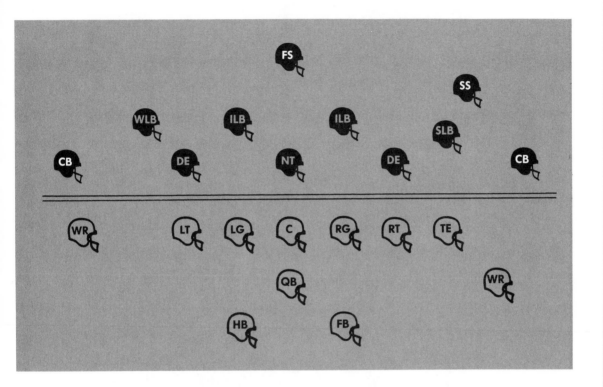

A corner must have good speed. He not only has to run fast straight ahead, but he also has to backpedal, and react to his left, right, up, or down with great quickness.

Size at cornerback isn't the most important thing, but you'd like him to be as large as possible while still having the quickness and agility to play the position.

The **free safety** is a smart guy with good range who plays deep and usually directs the defensive backfield. He's football's centerfielder, free to roam around. He has to be a good open field tackler, and that's the hardest kind of tackle to make. There are no sidelines in the middle of the field to help you ride a ball carrier out of bounds.

All-Pro defensive back Ronnie Lott can show you what life in the secondary is all about. When you're the last line of defense, you have to tackle one-on-one.

A free safety has to have the range to go from the middle of the field to either sideline, and he has to help the cornerbacks on deep passes.

The **strong safety** plays against the tight end. A strong safety is a defensive back when the offense passes, and he becomes another linebacker when they run. For that reason, you'd like him to be the largest guy in the secondary. The free safety can be almost any size; quickness in reacting to the ball is most important.

There are a lot of theories about how to cover a receiver. Some coaches tell their coverage guys to watch his belt buckle, eye, nose, ear, shoulder, or any other one thing. The idea is not to get faked out, not to let the receiver get you turned the wrong way. I always thought those theories were silly.

Why should a good athlete be watching a guy's nose? Why limit a good athlete to a belt buckle? I always told my people that the receiver coming out presents an image, and that whole image is what you cover.

There are three basic ways you can use all this defense whether you play 3-4 or 4-3: press, play normal, play soft.

By press, I mean that more players than your linemen will try to penetrate. If you have to make something happen, then you press. The advantage is you can cause a loss of yardage or a fumble. The disadvantage is if the offense breaks through, they'll get a bigger gain.

Normal or basic play means read and react. You play aggressively as always, but you don't charge.

Playing soft means playing your secondary and linebackers farther back than usual. You do this in long-yardage situations and when you're protecting a lead.

You play the game of defense just as you play offense. A team's personality is based on what you know and do the best. And that's exactly what you do, game after game.

My Kind
of
Fanatics:
Special Teams

Any time a kicker or punter is on the field, the special team guys are out there with him.

There's a simple difference between kicking and punting. Kicking is when the ball is on a tee or held by a guy on the ground. Punting is when the punter holds the ball himself.

A team kicks for field goals. They also kick to the opposing team at the start of the game, the start of the second half, and after scores. They punt to the opposing team on fourth down when they're not close enough for a field goal or a first down attempt.

The team that receives the ball *returns* it upfield while the team that kicked or punted *covers*. The returning team tries to gain as many yards as possible. The team covering the kick or punt tries to stop them.

Good coverage is very important. Return guys can be very dangerous. They have names like Anthony Carter and Darrell Green. In fact, Darrell's fifty-two-yard punt return in the 1988 play-offs helped put the Redskins in the Super Bowl. If your

Speed and agility: When Anthony Carter handles the ball, there's always the possibility of a big play.

coverage can pin the other team inside their 20-yard line, that's a big play. They're more than eighty yards from a touchdown and you've given your defense a big advantage.

When the offense has to play close to their own goal line, defense has them against a wall. And any turnover (a fumble recovered or an interception) down there means that *your* offense will take over the ball twenty yards or less from scoring.

On coverage, you just want the men to run down the field fast, knock guys down, and tackle the ball carrier.

I used to tell my players that special teams breed fanaticism. When we kick off and they're going down the field, we need eleven fanatics.

So then my guys started flying, hitting people anywhere, and forgetting to tackle the ball carrier. And worse, once the ball carrier did get tackled, the whistle would blow, and five fanatics would jump on him. The play's over, you can't do that.

Obviously, *fanaticism* wasn't quite the right word.

"Special teams are *controlled* fanatics," I told them. "You have to be a *controlled* fanatic, and after you tackle the guy with the ball, *stop* being a fanatic."

Punt coverage

The first thing a **punter** has to do is to receive the snap from the center, and that's not easy. The punter stands fifteen yards behind the line of scrimmage. The snap is like a fifteen-yard pass between the center's legs. Catching the ball cleanly is one of the most important things a punter does. The defense is rushing a punt, and if the punter bobbles the ball, he can get nailed.

Once the punt is made, the important thing is **hang time**. Hang time is how long the punted ball is in the air. It's the time that elapses beginning when the ball leaves the punter's foot and ending when it is caught. Anything over 4.3 seconds is a good hang time. The longer the ball's in the air, the more time your coverage has getting downfield.

Punting is a natural thing. Physical size doesn't help. Punters

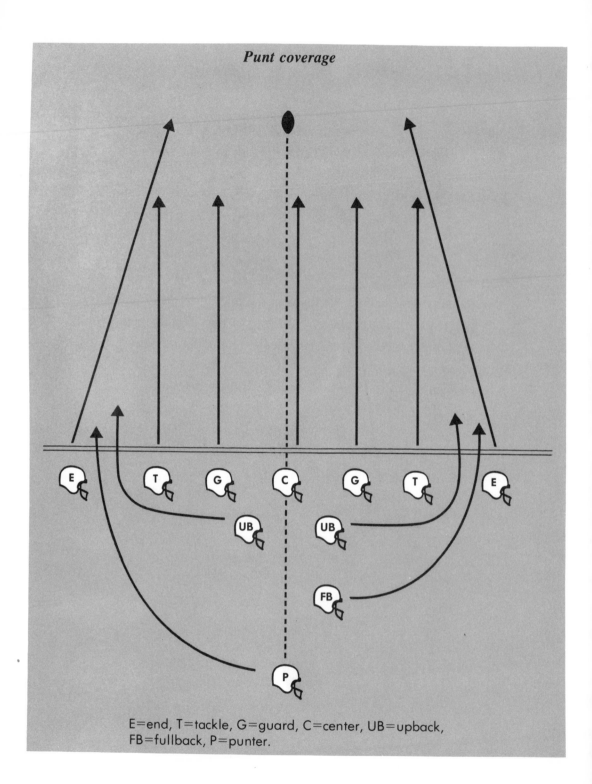

Punt coverage

E=end, T=tackle, G=guard, C=center, UB=upback,
FB=fullback, P=punter.

are like golfers. The little guys seem to boom the ball the farthest. And a punter's kick is as synchronized as the golfer's swing.

The punting team lines up a lot like the standard offense. All the players move downfield to cover the punt.

NFL rules allow only the two outside men, the two ends, to leave the line when the ball is snapped. Everyone else has to wait for the punt.

In the heat of the game, it's impossible for those eight players who remain on the line to actually hear the punt. And they can't turn around and watch it, either. I had my players judge the punt by counting, "One thousand one, one thousand two, one thousand three"; then they'd take off.

Each man on the coverage team has to get downfield as fast as he can. He closes in on the ball carrier while staying in a direct relationship to the teammates beside him. The coverage team goes, as a unit, to the left or right as the ball goes to the left or right.

Punt return

The basic punt return alignment has a six-man front line. Two outside men rush the punter to make sure the ball is kicked, so the punter doesn't try a trick play.

Nobody said you *have* to punt on fourth down, even when the punter is on the field. Since it's fourth down for the offense, the punter could take the snap and throw a pass to one of the ends. That's a trick play, and if a coach calls one he'd better be sure it'll be good. A coach looks like a genius when a trick works, but he sure looks dumb when it doesn't.

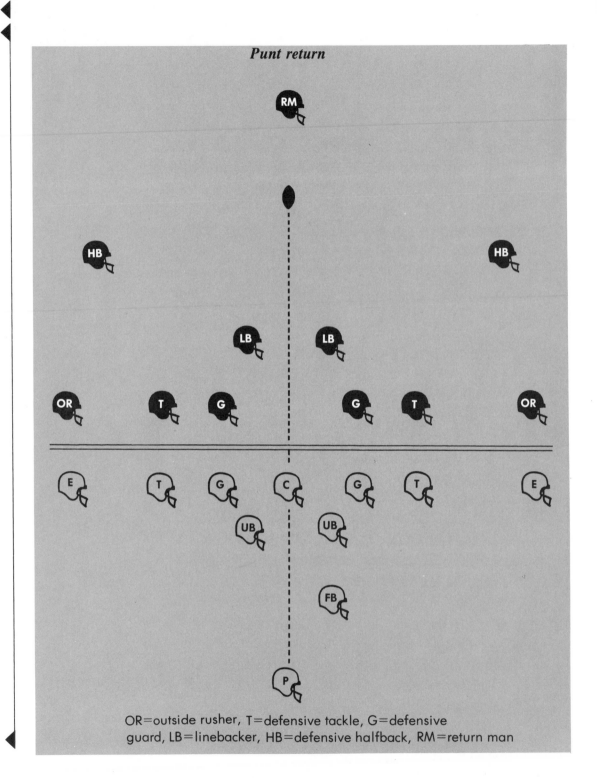

Punt return

OR=outside rusher, T=defensive tackle, G=defensive guard, LB=linebacker, HB=defensive halfback, RM=return man

Once the ball is punted, it becomes the return man's responsibility.

The **return man** has to be a guy who can catch anything that's kicked. That's the first priority. If he fumbles the punt, the other team could recover and be in great field position. After the catch, any yards he can gain upfield as a runner are a bonus.

A return man also has to have good judgment.

If the ball goes into the end zone, without being touched by the returning team, the ball is spotted at the 20-yard line. Twenty yards is probably farther than they could have gained with the coverage team flying toward them, so it's important that the return man know when to catch it and when to let it go.

On high or short punts, when the cover team is zeroing in before the return man has caught the ball, he should signal a fair catch. The ball is spotted where he caught it, and he gets to catch the ball without worrying about being hit and perhaps fumbling.

The kicking team: coverage and return

On a kickoff, the ball is placed on the 35-yard line. The kickoff team lines up on the 30-yard line.

The outside guys, the **fives**, on the kickoff line are the fastest. They're the contain men. They contain the ball carrier into the middle of the field. They try to funnel the ball carrier to their teammates, who can make a tackle. Usually, wide receivers or defensive backs are fives.

Kickoff coverage and return

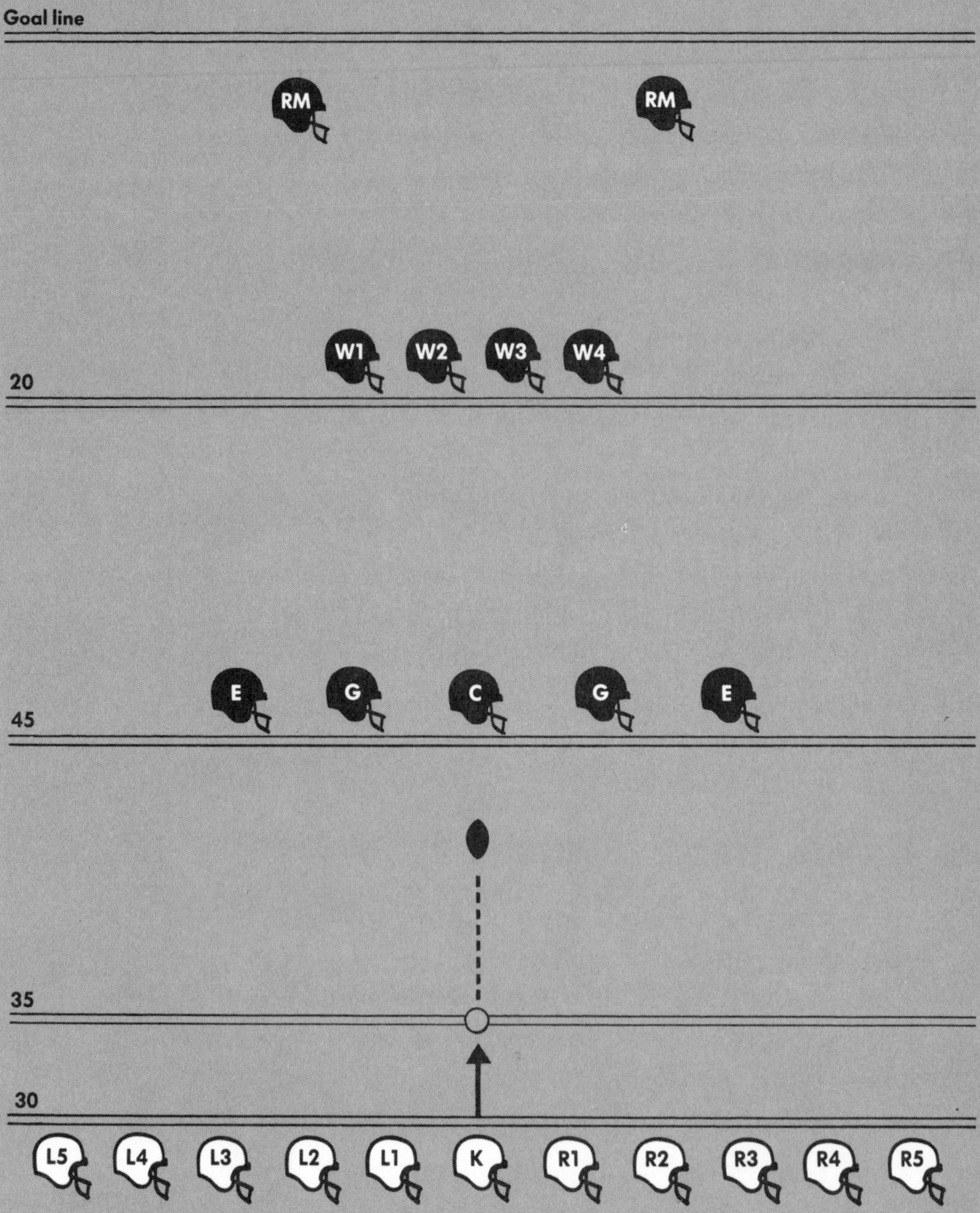

Goal line

RM · RM

W1 W2 W3 W4

20

E · G · C · G · E

45

35

30

L5 L4 L3 L2 L1 K R1 R2 R3 R4 R5

A **kicker** needs to get good hang time. Hang time is as important on a kick as it is on a punt. A good kick gives the cover team time to get downfield.

On the return team, the first line of ends, guards, and center are nimble blockers. They have to be nimble because the coverage team running toward them are fast-moving targets.

The **wedge**, the Ws, should be linebackers, tight ends, or fullbacks—big people who can handle the ball on short kicks if they have to.

The return men are fast running backs, wide receivers, or defensive backs.

There are usually three types of returns: middle, left, and right. On a middle return, your front five block the ones and twos on the opposing team. Your wedge blocks the threes, and you have two wedge men free to lead the ball up the middle.

On left and right returns, your front five block the returning threes, twos, and ones. Then your wedge end men take the fours and fives. You try to start the ball up the middle and then turn it out to the left or right.

Field goals

When the offense is going for a field goal or an extra point, the defense is rushing. Big defensive linemen get their arms up, trying to deflect the kick. The offensive line is blocking them.

In the NFL, the kick is made with the ball on the ground. In college football, they use a tee.

The **holder** (kneeling seven yards back from the line) takes the snap from the center, puts an end down, and holds the top with his index finger. He rotates the ball so that the laces face away from the kicker. And he does all that in one smooth motion.

A good punter can be a real weapon for the defense. Sean Landetta of the Giants pins teams deep in their own territory all the time.

The basics of kicking are the same whether it's straight-ahead or soccer style. You keep your head down, you watch the ball, and you kick through it.

Kickers, like punters, don't have to be big guys. And also like punters, they have very few attempts in a game, compared to their teammates. They live with instant pressure. On field goals and extra points, the kicker's job is to get the ball up and through the posts. They have to come off the bench and do their jobs well.

No NFL team in history has been good without having good special teams. They're my kind of fanatics.

PART 3

The
Pro
Game

Winning and Losing, What You'll See, and Ways to Watch

Fans want their team to get ahead, to score, to win, and that's a great game. But if you're just a fan of football, the best game to see is between two great teams playing for a championship.

The next best is, during the season, when two good teams are trying to get to a championship.

The third best is when a top team is playing an average team. There could be an upset.

Upsets happen because players have pride. Even when a team has lost ten in a row, the players truly believe they're going to win the next one. If a player didn't have that kind of pride, he never would have made it to the NFL in the first place.

It's always a more exciting game if the team that's not supposed to win scores first. You wonder, can they keep the lead, or will the other team come back?

A good game has everything: long passes, long runs, good defense that stops a drive on third down and short yardage, good kicking, and few penalties.

A lot of penalties slow down a game and mar it. You can't

get in the flow when the team lunges and stops all the time. You can't get in the flow as a fan, as a player, as a coach, as a broadcaster. No one gets in the flow.

Penalties aren't fun. They can kill a drive. Avoiding penalties is one thing a team has to do to win.

There are a number of other things that go into a victory. The big play is important, but that's not all.

One of the biggest factors is what's called **turnover ratio**. A turnover is a fumble recovered or an interception. If my team gives up three turnovers and doesn't get any, then it'll be hard for us to win. But if we give up three turnovers and get three, we're even and we have a chance.

Another big factor in winning and losing, and a factor that no one likes, is injuries.

Today's professional players are bigger, stronger, faster, and more talented than ever before. But as the players have improved and grown, the size of the field is the same as it was a century ago.

A field is 53⅓ yards wide and 120 yards long (including the end zones). There are a lot of big, hard-hitting, strong men playing games in the same space smaller men played in years ago. In the NFL today, piles develop on the field and big guys collide.

Some of them are going to get hurt and that's going to affect a team. It may even affect a season. Fortunately, few of the injuries are serious. And I honestly believe that *intentional* violence is not what causes injuries. The NFL wouldn't allow it. It's not good for the game.

I don't know what can be done to reduce injuries. The playing field isn't going to be enlarged, and players aren't going to get smaller and less talented. It has just become a part of the game nobody likes.

A team that stays healthy, that doesn't lose the ball when they're on offense, and has strength everywhere on the field, is a team that could go all the way to the Super Bowl. But you still never know.

NFL teams are up against some of the strongest competition in professional sports. To have a fighting chance, you need well-executed strategy throughout a game. Strategy, for offense or defense, means to map out a plan of attack.

Any quarterback and any coach can eat up any defense if they know what's coming. And if a good defense knows what the offense will do, they'll eat *them* up.

So the big thing both sides will do is make you *think* you're going to get something, show it to you, then, *boom*, do something else.

If there was one play, one formation, one kind of assignment that could work everytime, they'd just do one thing the whole game. But unless you find a weakness on the opposing team, you need a mixture of things to win.

When the quarterback goes into the huddle, he calls the formation, the play, the blocking, and the snap count. To save time, everything is coded in numbers and one-syllable words.

"Far right eighteen bob odd oh on three," for example, is the kind of thing you'd hear in a huddle. It tells each player what to do.

In my Raider huddle, "far right" told the players where to line up; "eighteen" meant that the halfback would carry the ball on a sweep around the right end; "bob" told the fullback to block the linebacker outside the right end; "odd" told the linemen which way to block and for the right guard to pull and lead the way for the halfback; "oh" told the left guard to follow the right guard; "on three" is the snap count, when everyone is to start moving.

When the offense lines up, the quarterback usually calls out audibles. "Blue thirty-two, blue thirty-two," or something. Those audibles can change a play or call an adjustment to something the quarterback sees in the defense. Audibles can also be fake signals to throw the defense off.

While this is happening, there's another guy calling signals on defense. Usually he's the middle or inside linebacker. He calls for adjustments his side should make.

A coach can call for a certain kind of defense, but he can't know the offensive formation before they line up. Once the offense gets into a formation, the defense has to make changes based on what's coming at them.

The defense mixes things up by going into zone coverage, man-to-man, blitzing, or any combination of defenses. Any kind of mixture to keep the offense from knowing what to expect.

A blitz, for example, can be a very effective defensive play. Blitzing means that a linebacker or defensive back charges instead of waiting for a play to happen. The idea is to take control by stopping the play before it gets started.

When a blitz works, the linebacker or safety comes crashing

The snap is where it all begins. Center Don Mosebar of the Raiders prepares to snap the ball to the quarterback.

through the line of scrimmage and tackles the quarterback or running back before the play can develop. But if the quarterback reads the blitz properly, and his linemen do their job of blocking, the quarterback can attack.

Blitzing makes it easier for a receiver to get open. On a standard three-man rush, eight defenders are left to cover receivers. The quarterback has to throw the ball through a forest of coverage. When there's an eight-man blitz, the quarterback has to get rid of the ball more quickly, but there's no forest downfield. There are only three men on defense left to cover the receivers.

Given good blocking against a blitz, it's easier to complete a pass, and it could be a big play for long yardage.

The threat of a blitz, a fake blitz, can be as effective as the real thing. If the defense acts as if it's going to blitz, then drops back, the quarterback might throw a quick pass into the middle of the field that the defense will intercept.

Or how about a *fake* fake blitz? The quarterback *thinks* the defense is going to drop back from a fake blitz, and he sends everybody out. Surprise! Here comes the defense, no one gets blocked, *ploomm!*

That may give you some idea of what's on a player's, and coach's, mind during a game.

The important thing to remember about football strategy is this: with just eleven guys to work with, no matter what play, formation, or assignment you call, there's always *something* that you're giving up. There's always going to be a weakness somewhere.

When you blitz, you're giving up receiver coverage. When you don't blitz, you give the offense more time to set up a play, or to pick up short yardage on a run. Whenever you do one thing, you're giving up something else. But that's what you have to do. And that's another one of those things that makes football so tremendously exciting.

There are different ways to watch football and see all this in action.

When you watch a game on television, the camera shows you

where the ball is, and most of the time you can tell what's going to happen. At a live game, though, if you want to know where the ball is, and where it's going, the worst guy to watch is the quarterback.

The quarterback is paid not to let you know what's going to happen. If you know what's going to happen from watching the quarterback, the defense will watch him too. So he's going to fake, he's going to reverse pivot, he's not going to let you see the ball.

Watch the center. His snap is the first thing that can happen. Then watch the two guys beside him, the two guards.

The first thing that can happen after the ball is snapped is a line block. Then a handoff can happen. And the *last* thing that can happen is a pass.

Those middle guys on the offensive line are the first to do something. Everyone else can wait.

If the center and guards fire out, it's going to be an inside run, a run on the inside of the line. If a guard pulls, if he blocks a man from the side, it's going to be a run to that side. If they drop back for pass protection, it's going to be a pass. And if you see it's going to be a pass, you can look for the receivers.

You can also see the same kinds of things by watching the defense.

If you want to know where the ball is going, and you want to watch the defense, keep an eye on the middle linebacker. If he goes one way after the snap, that's the way the ball is going. If he goes back, it's going to be a pass. He's paid to know where to move.

So if you want to know where the ball is going, watch the middle of the offense, or the middle of the defense. That's where the action will start, and what they do will direct you to what's going to happen. That's the advantage of going to a game—you can choose what to watch instead of what the television camera shows you.

There's another way to watch a game. It's how I used to watch football.

I wanted to be a lineman, so I watched them on every play. I'd look at everything else that was going on too, but I would pick out who I wanted to be and watch the game through his eyes.

When you really watch someone, you realize what a tough job he has. You'll see that nothing he does is easy or simple.

The center, for instance, has a big responsibility. He has to do the same things that the other offensive linemen do. He has to block man-on-man and help double-team a rusher. Some teams have even started to have their centers pull. There's all that *plus* he has to snap the ball. He has to get the ball to the quarterback exactly when it's supposed to be snapped.

Say the snap count is "on three." When the offense lines up, the quarterback will call the audibles and then go, "Set . . . hut . . . hut . . . hut!" Everybody on offense moves just after the *t* in the third "hut."

If the center snaps the ball too soon, he'll be the only guy moving on offense. But the defense isn't waiting for a snap count. They just watch the ball. They move when it moves. On an early

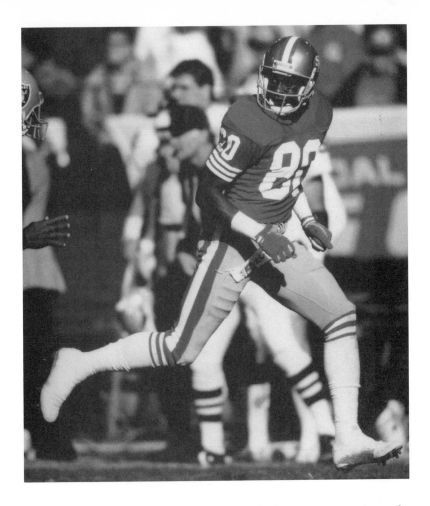

One way to watch the game is to watch the guys away from the ball. If you see it's going to be a pass, look for the receivers— like Jerry Rice of the 49ers.

snap, here comes the defense and *boom*, a lot of offensive linemen are going to be knocked on their seats.

If he snaps late, though, the other offensive linemen will be moving while the center's sitting there with the ball. The offense is going to be offsides, and that's a five-yard penalty. Losing five yards because you were offsides can be the difference between a scoring drive and having to punt on fourth down. And it also makes you look stupid.

So the center has all that responsibility, and as if that weren't enough, there's a 250-pound, 6-foot nose tackle on top of him, ready to attack.

Nose tackles show no mercy for a guy who's doing a tough job already. That nose tackle will attack the center's snapping shoulder if the center doesn't get his hands up in time to block.

What you'll see in a good center, Jay Hilgenberg of the Bears, for instance, is a snap on the money and then a winning battle against the defensive tackle.

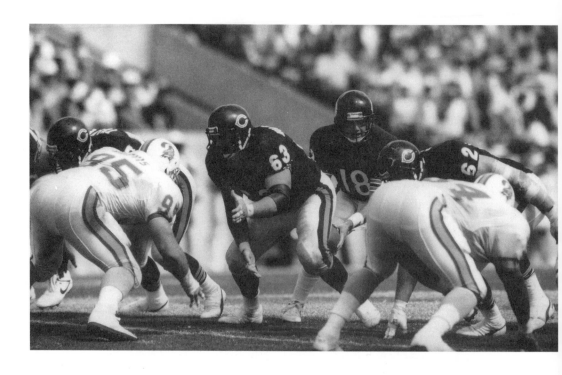

Snap the ball and get the hands up in time to block—a center's job isn't easy, but Jay Hilgenberg of the Bears does it all.

Quickness is the thing to watch in a center. Snapping the ball and not letting the snap get you beat. Some centers are so nervous about blocking that they get a head start by snapping the ball early. But the other offensive linemen will want to kill him. If he snaps early, the guard next to him may get beat and everybody will be looking at him, but it was the center's fault. He caused the whole thing.

The line protecting a quarterback has to be good because quarterback is the most important position on the field. One thing that makes an offensive lineman good, or any player anywhere on the field, is footwork.

Feet are probably the most important thing in football. Good feet will beat bad feet every time. And in blocking, bad feet will kill you.

If your feet are in a bad position, you can't do anything. On pass blocking, for instance, a right tackle will keep his left foot (his inside foot) forward and his right foot (his outside foot) back.

There's a good reason why he does.

If his inside foot is forward, that's where his strength is, and he's protecting the direct route to the quarterback. He can block a defensive end on pass protection, ride him all the way to the outside, and he won't be able to get back in.

But if the tackle's inside foot is back, he doesn't have any strength on that side of his body. The defense will move inside on him, and get the passer. And there's nothing you can do once the defense goes sailing past.

When you watch a quarterback, you'll see what he does with his arm. That's the obvious thing. But look for his footwork, too.

A quarterback's feet have to be darn near shoulder width all the time. If they are, when one foot moves, the other foot has to move. And the hips have to be open so he can rotate and throw.

If his feet are spread out wide, he can't make a quick move either way. He can't throw, he can't rotate his hips, he can't do a thing.

Watch how a quarterback handles the ball, how quickly he drops back, how quickly he releases the ball, and all the different moves he makes on passes downfield and handoffs to his backs.

And watch those runnng backs. Running plays are important, but in the NFL, running isn't the only key to winning the game. Teams with good running attacks do have an advantage, though. If your team can run, not only can you pick up a lot of first downs running the ball, but you're able to fake the run and throw the pass.

When a quarterback fakes a handoff to a guy like Herschel Walker, the defense thinks, *"Holy Toledo!"* and runs forward to stop him. And that's going to leave receivers wide open. This kind of fake is called **play action**.

A team without a good running game can't do that. The quarterback will fake to a back, and nobody will care.

An offense that can fake a defensive player out of position has an enormous advantage. Getting even one guy out of the way can open up a hole. And taking advantage of those gaps is a big part of playing offense.

For running backs, reading the defense, knowing how and where to leave the line, is a crucial skill. A running back has to see everything while he's running with the ball. The better and faster he reads the defense, the more yards he's going to get.

You can also see a running back *misread* the defense and his

Running back Barry Sanders of the Lions finds a hole in the defense and wards off a tackler.

blocking by hitting the wrong hole. He'll come up the loser. Or you'll see him run behind a pulling guard, then leave his blocking too soon. He'll lose again.

When you watch a good running back, you'll see football instincts in action. And you'll also see great instincts when you watch the defense.

I've said that a strong safety is part defensive back and part linebacker. If the offense runs the ball, he has to get up there to support the tacklers. He has to be able to take on a sweep, force it back in, and make a play. Maybe even take on a guard.

If it's a pass play, he has to get in pass coverage, either zone or man-to-man.

When you watch a strong safety, you'll see how quickly he reads the play, how quickly he gets toward the line of scrimmage on a run, how quickly he gets back on a pass, and how quickly he knows what to do.

Sooner or later, everyone on defense will know whether it's a pass or a run. But the better the player, the quicker he'll know.

The average player will know at a rate of *thousand-one boom*, it's a pass. The good player will know, *boom*, it's a pass.

Recognizing what's coming is the first step. But *just* recognizing it is not going to help you.

A coach, through watching hundreds of games, will be able to recognize a pass when the play starts. What's he going to do about it? Jump up and down? Wave his arms? None of the players are watching the coach once the play starts, and it would be too late anyway if they did.

A great defensive player is someone who can tell what the offense is doing and do something to stop it immediately. Ever notice that great players always seem to be in the middle of every play? That's no accident. That's not luck. They see and they go. That's what makes them great.

And great defensive players don't get suckered.

Sometimes only the coach knows when a man got suckered out of a play. Any time a deep pass is completed in the middle, for example, and it's not a blitz, the free safety fouled up. The cornerback who was supposed to cover the receiver will get the blame, but the safety probably was faked out of the play. He thought the play was going somewhere else; he bit on a fake.

Players have to be smart. You'll see that when you watch any position. A football player has to know his plays, his reactions, and what the man he's playing against is trying to do. He has to be aware of the down, distance, the score, the rules.

That, to me, is smart. When it's third down and inches, you can't jump offsides. That's dumb.

Players have to know what the other team is doing every minute of the game, where their teammates are, where they can get help on a play. That's smart.

To be successful, you can't do dumb things, at least not often.

In the huddle, when the quarterback calls the formation, the play, the blocking, and the snap count, that's a lot for a person to remember. But that's what they're paid to do. Pros don't have to go to school, or to a job; they don't have to do anything except play football.

But sometimes a player forgets what the quarterback called. In a game, if you see offensive linemen talking after a huddle, they probably forgot the play.

Even the quarterback can forget what he just called.

In Super Bowl VIII, Miami was on Minnesota's 5-yard line. Miami's quarterback, Bob Griese, got behind his center, Jim Langer. Griese looked over the defense, and then just couldn't remember the snap count.

He turned to his running backs, Larry Csonka and Jim Kiick, lined up behind him.

"Hey, Zonk, what's it on?" he said.

Csonka said, "On two." But then Kiick yelled, "No, it's on one." Csonka yelled back, "No, it's on two!"

So here was Miami, trying to win the Super Bowl, debating the snap count on the 5-yard line. Griese called some signals, Langer snapped on one, Csonka jumped, Griese handed off, Csonka plowed, touchdown Miami.

If you do something dumb, it sure pays to be smart.

Hall-of-Fame fullback Larry Csonka drags tacklers for another Miami first down.

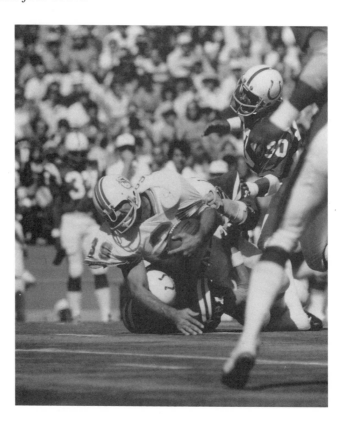

★ ★ ★

When you watch a game through a player's eyes, you'll see that pro football is not all running long runs, or catching long passes, or sacking the quarterback. It's not all glory, but that makes the glory, when it comes, even greater.

Down and Distance: Packages and Plays

I once asked Vince Lombardi what makes a good coach.

Lombardi was the coach of the Green Bay Packer powerhouse teams, one of the greatest coaches in football history.

"The best coaches," he said, "know what the end result will look like, whether it's an offensive play, a defense coverage, or any other area. If you don't know what the end result is supposed to look like, you'll never get there. Bad coaches don't know what the heck they want. Good coaches do."

After that, whenever I designed a play for my Raider teams, I always started with a mental picture of the end result. And then I worked to create that result.

When you see a play on paper, it's a bunch of circles and triangles and lines, and that's not always easy to understand.

But, hey, nothing is easy until you know what it's all about.

Diagrams are used to give players the whole picture of a play—what the whole thing should look like. Players have to understand what the play is supposed to accomplish, and they have to know the mechanics of the play before they can try it.

Coaching isn't rah-rah, "win it for the Gipper" halftime

"Good coaches know what they want. Bad coaches don't." Hall-
of-Famer Vince Lombardi, coach of the powerhouse Green Bay
Packer teams, was one of the best.

speeches. Coaching is really teaching. We'd teach the plays,
draw it on the blackboard, show it to the players on film. The
players would have a picture in their minds, and then we'd go
out on the field.

First, you walk through the play. Then you practice it at half speed. The last step is running through it at full speed, man-to-man, against another player.

You don't diagram a play and then have your twenty-two guys do it at full speed. When the players don't do it well, the coach will think, "That doesn't work." What a coach must remember is that his players have to learn it, and they learn it slowly.

Even a pro isn't going to do a new play well the first time. He learns it, repeats it, repeats it, repeats it.

Professional football was once a game of eleven guys playing against eleven guys on every down, all day long. When there was a mismatch between offensive and defensive players, you'd have that mismatch for the whole game. If their left defensive tackle was better than my right offensive tackle, I had to get a tight end or running back in there to help on every play.

One of the biggest strategic rule changes in football history came about in the 1940s, with refinements added ever since. In today's professional football, there is free substitution. There always have to be eleven players on the field before the snap, but while the ball is dead, coaches can take players out and send in substitute players for even a single play.

Football today is a game of down and distance. You have to drive for a score. It's great if your quarterback can throw a seventy-yard touchdown on second down, but that's pretty rare.

Mostly, an offense keeps driving all the way to the goal line by getting first downs. Let's say you're starting at your own 20-yard line. It's first down and ten. A running play might pick up two yards. Now it's second and eight, from your own 22.

The quarterback calls a pass play, a wide receiver goes downfield, but the cornerback bats down the ball. Now its *third* and eight. And you're still on your 22.

What would you do? You've got eight yards to go for a first down. Will you try for a short-pass play? Another long pass? Try to run for those eight yards? If you don't gain eight yards, where will you be? *Fourth* down.

Whatever you decide *has* to get that first down unless you want those fanatics on special teams to take the field.

You're in a tough spot. You're seventy-eight yards away from the goal. You're out of field goal range (a field goal from forty yards away is a darn good kick). You have to pick up a first down *now* or punt to the opposing team on fourth down.

A team isn't likely to try for eight yards on fourth down in that situation. It's too dangerous. If you don't get the yards for a first down, the opposing team will take over the ball on your 22-yard line. They're twenty-two yards from your goal. You don't want that, so you'd punt and let the fanatics loose.

When you're in a situation where a first down is crucial, you want the best possible guys on the field to get it for you. You want what coaches call the best possible "package."

And that's what NFL strategy is based on. The down, the distance from a first down and the goal line, and keeping the drive alive by getting players in the game to get the job done.

Simple enough, maybe, but one thing complicates this: Offense isn't the only side that can substitute. The defense is going to react to your substitutions by making substitutions on their side.

On a strategic level, football is really more than just a game of my plays against your plays and my offense against your defense. It's my *different* offenses, my situational players, against your *different* defenses, your situational players.

This isn't simple stuff, and there just isn't any way to make it simple. But I hope I can at least make it understandable. Keep in mind, too, that this isn't stuff you *have* to know. You can enjoy watching a game without knowing a nickelback from a pretzel vendor. But you might enjoy it more if you do.

Down and distance

FIRST DOWN AND TEN

On first down, the starting players are on the field. These are the "base" players I talked about in the offense chapter. Five linemen, a tight end, two wide receivers, two backs, and a quarterback, usually. Some teams use a base of two tight ends, two wide receivers, and one running back.

A team might use a two tight-end base if they're facing a dangerous weak side linebacker. When there's a tight end on both sides of the line, in theory, there's no weak side. Nice theory, but it doesn't work if that second tight end can't block.

First down can be a running or passing down. At the start of a game, on first down when the Raiders had the ball, I always called a running play. I wanted everybody to relax by making hits and getting their uniforms dirty. But throughout a game, a mixture of running and passing on first down works best.

There's greater pressure in the later downs to pick up yardage, but if you can be successful on first down, you have a big advantage. There'll be fewer yards to gain on the rest of your downs.

To me, a good first down performance means picking up five yards or more. It is then possible to go for a big play on second down.

SECOND OR THIRD AND LONG YARDAGE: PASSING DOWNS

On second or third down and long yardage, the coach will go to his long-yardage "package," players who are capable of different things.

A long-yardage package has more wide receivers and fewer backs and tight ends. If you send in an extra wide receiver, you take out either one back or a tight end. Now you have three wide receivers on offense. If you want four wide receivers, you take out still another back or tight end.

A pass is much more effective in picking up long yardage than a run. Almost any completed pass is going to get you a first down, while a run is easier for the defense to stop short.

If you need good receivers on the field, you're better off not trying to fool the defense by keeping running backs in the game. You need guys running patterns downfield, putting pressure on the coverage, and getting open.

Meanwhile, the defense is reacting to your changes.

On first down they play their base against your base, whether their base defense is a 4-3 or 3-4 formation.

Then when the offense goes to a long-yardage package of an extra wide receiver, the defense needs an extra defensive back to cover him.

Remember that the defensive base has four defensive backs (two safeties and two cornerbacks). When the defense brings in a *fifth* defensive back, that's called a nickel package, and the fifth defense back is called a nickelback.

Whom does a nickelback replace? Usually, they'll take out a linebacker and keep their pass rush at three or four linemen.

If the offense brings in *more* wide receivers, the defense needs even more defensive backs to cover them.

A defensive dime package brings in a fifth and sixth defensive back, who replace two linebackers. A quarter package brings in a fifth, sixth, and seventh additional defensive back in place of three linebackers.

You'll see all this substituting going on in a game when guys are coming and going left and right from the sidelines.

If you didn't see substitutes come in, you might be able to see the extra wide receivers just by looking at the offensive formation.

When the offense has brought in more wide receivers, they might go into a shotgun formation. For a fan, the shotgun is one of the easiest formations to spot because the quarterback is standing back from the center, about five yards back from the line of scrimmage.

The shotgun goes with substitution because it's built for wide receivers. Some teams don't use the shotgun at all, though, and still accomplish the same thing.

SECOND AND SHORT YARDAGE

Second down and short is a good time to take a shot at a big play. If it doesn't work, it'll be third and short and you can pick up a first down on a running play.

THIRD AND SHORT YARDAGE: A RUNNING DOWN

On third down and short yardage, the coach will go for his short-yardage package. That includes two or three tight ends, and fewer wide receivers.

If you take out wide receivers, the defense will take out defensive backs. When the offense has three tight ends, the defense will match that with extra safeties or linebackers.

Goal-line plays are where games are won and lost. Here the Giants' Pepper Johnson loses his helmet in the pileup.

ANY DOWN AND GOAL

Goal-line plays are probably the most important plays of all. We used to practice goal-line plays at least half an hour every day, both offense and defense. The goal line is where games are won and lost.

The game is different down there. The field is shorter, you only have a yard or so to work with—and knowing how to make that go in your favor takes a lot of practice.

If your offense can score every time you get to the goal line, and if your defense can stop the opposing team from scoring most times, you have a huge advantage.

On the goal line, the winner will be the team who wins the battle of the pile.

Down there, it's toe-to-toe. The ball's snapped, *boom*, the two lines become one big pile. If the pile pushes forward, touchdown. If the pile is pushed back, the defense did its job. No touchdown.

Distance from the goal line

Goal-line plays are one example of how field position—your distance from the goal—influences plays and packages. Field position, in addition to downs, plays a major part in plays—up and down the field.

A football field can be divided into five major areas. The *plus* side of the field is your opponent's side of the 50-yard line, the area your offense attacks on the way to a score. The *minus* side is your side of the 50, the area your defense protects and the area your offense moves away from. Here is the way it breaks down:

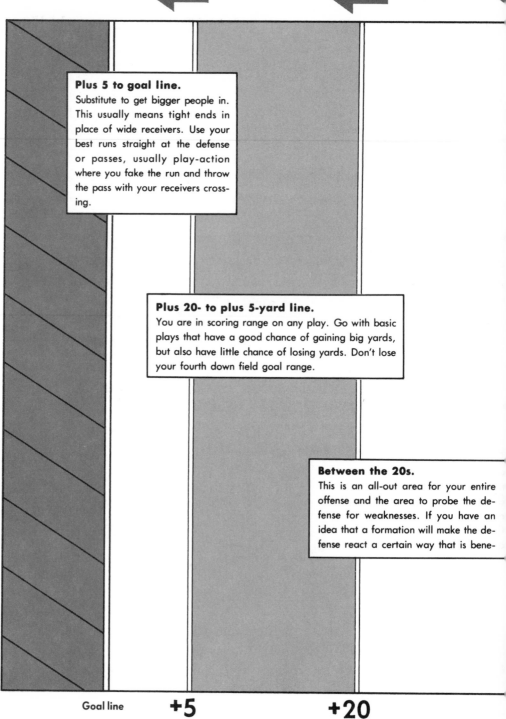

Plus 5 to goal line.
Substitute to get bigger people in. This usually means tight ends in place of wide receivers. Use your best runs straight at the defense or passes, usually play-action where you fake the run and throw the pass with your receivers crossing.

Plus 20- to plus 5-yard line.
You are in scoring range on any play. Go with basic plays that have a good chance of gaining big yards, but also have little chance of losing yards. Don't lose your fourth down field goal range.

Between the 20s.
This is an all-out area for your entire offense and the area to probe the defense for weaknesses. If you have an idea that a formation will make the defense react a certain way that is bene-

Goal line **+5** **+20**

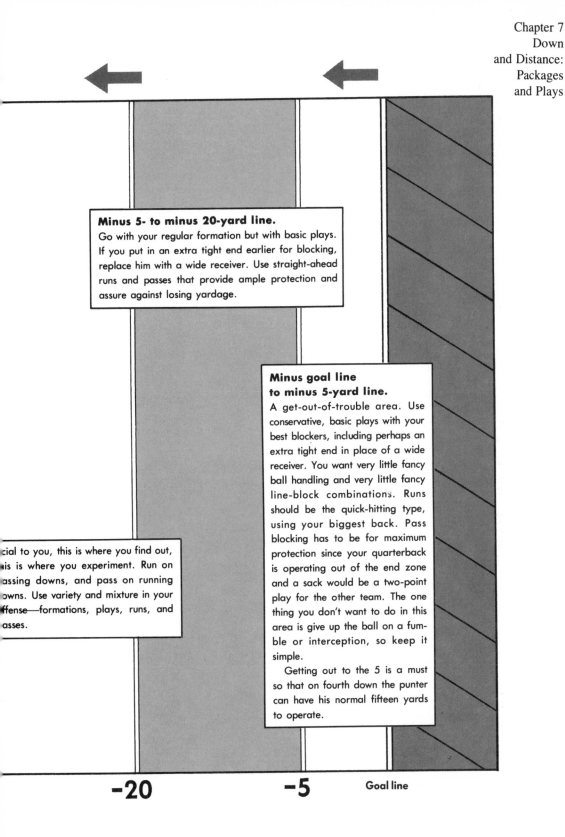

Minus 5- to minus 20-yard line.
Go with your regular formation but with basic plays.
If you put in an extra tight end earlier for blocking,
replace him with a wide receiver. Use straight-ahead
runs and passes that provide ample protection and
assure against losing yardage.

**Minus goal line
to minus 5-yard line.**
A get-out-of-trouble area. Use
conservative, basic plays with your
best blockers, including perhaps an
extra tight end in place of a wide
receiver. You want very little fancy
ball handling and very little fancy
line-block combinations. Runs
should be the quick-hitting type,
using your biggest back. Pass
blocking has to be for maximum
protection since your quarterback
is operating out of the end zone
and a sack would be a two-point
play for the other team. The one
thing you don't want to do in this
area is give up the ball on a fumble or interception, so keep it
simple.
    Getting out to the 5 is a must
so that on fourth down the punter
can have his normal fifteen yards
to operate.

cial to you, this is where you find out,
is is where you experiment. Run on
assing downs, and pass on running
owns. Use variety and mixture in your
ffense—formations, plays, runs, and
asses.

-20   **-5**   **Goal line**

As you know, the defense will be adjusting their strategy each time the offensive strategy changes. The defense will press, play normal, soft, man-to-man, zone, blitz, and substitute depending on offensive field position, down, distance, situation, and offensive substitution.

There really isn't such a thing as first string or second string in the NFL anymore. Beyond the starters, everyone has a job today. He's a short-yardage guy, he's a long-yardage guy, he's a third wide receiver, he's a special teams guy, he's a nickelback.

That's how pro football is played today.

Making It in the NFL [and Other Ways to Have a Life in Football]

When you're young and playing sports, there will be times when you feel discouraged. But if playing's fun, don't give up. There are too many stories of a guy who didn't make the team in the ninth grade and then grew up to be a superstar.

I once taught PE in elementary school. There was a kid in the class who I gave a C. The kid was growing fast and he was kind of awkward. His parents complained that he had all As and Bs except for that C. I said there's nothing wrong with it. He's not very good in PE.

The same kid went on to be a high school basketball star; he played at UCLA, and on to the pros. But when he was in my PE class, he earned a C.

A kid who's growing, a kid who's going to be really big, will be very awkward in elementary school. Sometimes those kids don't fully mature physically until they get into college. When you're young, your body is changing a lot.

There's a guy named Terry Long who started at right guard for the Pittsburgh Steelers. When he got out of high school, he weighed 160 pounds.

Then he went into the armed services, and when he came out he had grown a half-inch and gained 112 pounds.

Right out of high school, people would have laughed at him if he'd said, "I'm going to be a guard in the NFL." But he made it.

There may come a time when playing isn't fun anymore, even when you still love football. You should know that there are other ways to stay with the sport all your life.

Being a manager, a broadcaster, a photographer, a writer, or even a fan—there are so many ways to still be a part of the game without playing football yourself.

There are coaches who weren't good players. They just studied the game and dedicated their time to becoming coaches.

On television, you have a play-by-play guy and an analyst. Most of the analysts were players or coaches, but most of the play-by-play guys weren't. My partner, Pat Summerall, is an exception. He was a player in college in Arkansas and he was a player for the Giants and Cardinals in the NFL.

But most broadcasters and journalists were the type who really loved sports, got to a point where they couldn't play it anymore, and then went to something else. There are many more jobs *around* football than *in* football.

Making it to the pros isn't easy. There are great, good, and average players in the NFL, but there aren't any bad players. With only twenty-eight NFL teams and forty-five to fifty players on each, a player who can't get the job done is going to be replaced.

Chapter 8
Making It
in the NFL
(and Other Ways
to Have a Life
in Football)

The best players are always the ones who work harder than anybody else. They concentrate more, they know the most because they're the best listeners. And they are the "luckiest," too.

A great receiver like Fred Biletnikoff, one of my Raiders and now a member of the Hall of Fame, made what people always called "lucky" catches. But when you see a guy being lucky for fourteen *years*, you realize that the guy makes his own luck, through practice and alertness.

Even though it's not easy making it to the NFL, the road is all laid out for you. There's no mysterious or magical way it will happen. Here's how it works.

The good players in the sandlots play junior varsity football in high school. The good JV players move up to the varsity team. Then the good varsity players play in college—and the best of them go on to play in the pros.

There's no other way to do it. There's no way to jump from high school to the NFL.

So even though getting to the pros isn't easy, at least it's very simple. If you dream about playing in the NFL, all you have to do is take things one step at a time. Concentrate on playing your best at the level you're on. If you move up to college, there's a good chance you could make it all the way. When you play in college, every NFL team will be watching.

The pros have a scouting report on every college senior who plays football in the United States. It doesn't matter what size your school is or where it is—the pros will have a report on you.

Teams use those scouting reports to draft college players for the NFL.

Everyone is scouted. Where you go to college doesn't matter. The big stars don't always come from the big schools, but you *do* have to play.

The college draft is very important because teams pick the players; the players don't pick their team. In high school and college, it's possible to be a "walk-on," to try out for the team and make it. But there are very, very few walk-ons in the NFL.

Being a draft pick, though, doesn't mean you've made it. A draft pick is now officially an NFL rookie, but that's just the first step toward making it as a pro.

The toughest thing for any rookie is training camp, before the start of a new football season. In training camp, all day long, you never know what's coming up next. As a rookie, you've never been there before.

You practice in the morning, and you don't know what will come after practice or what the coaches will have you do in the afternoon practice. And, even worse, you never know if you'll be cut from the team.

A typical rookie's day starts at six in the morning. He has breakfast, then he goes to the training room to have his ankles taped.

Underneath their pads, players wear tape that helps provide extra support. Every player has to be taped, or he'll be fined.

A training camp will have over a hundred players. That's over two hundred ankles to be taped by the trainers.

Chapter 8
Making It
in the NFL
(and Other Ways
to Have a Life
in Football)

So the rookies get up at six, have breakfast, get their ankles taped. The veterans have their taping scheduled for around eight-thirty. The rookies have to sit around until all the players are taped, and then everybody goes out to practice at nine o'clock.

Morning practice usually lasts two or three hours. When it's over, everyone takes a shower and removes their tape. Then they have lunch. There's usually some meeting after lunch, then back to get taped again for the afternoon practice.

Afternoon practice starts around three and is over around five-thirty. There's dinner, and usually a meeting at seven o'clock or seven-thirty. The evening meeting usually goes to nine or nine-thirty.

After the last meeting, in a normal day at training camp, a guy has about an hour and a half or two hours of free time. Camp has an eleven o'clock curfew, and everyone starts the whole schedule again the next morning.

On top of coping with all that, a rookie has to learn his team's offense or defense and the plays, *and* he's got the pressure of competing for a job.

Let's say he's a wide receiver. He might be one of twelve wide receivers in the camp. Four of them played on the team last season, and the team is only going to *have* four.

A rookie has to perform well and learn. And if he's not a first or second draft choice, nobody will be rooting for him. He has to compete against veterans for their jobs. He gets tired, hurt, and sore. But if he can survive the camp, if he can make the team, then everything else he has to go through is easier.

Once a rookie goes through training camp, plays in four pre-season games, and makes the team, he has gotten a lot out of those couple of months. He's really not a rookie anymore.

A player really makes it in the NFL by degrees. The next goal,

Your football life doesn't get any better than winning the Super Bowl. I know, because I was the Raiders' coach when we won it all in Super Bowl XI.

Chapter 8
Making It
in the NFL
(and Other Ways
to Have a Life
in Football)

after making the team, is to be named a starting player. Then the goal is to be named an All-Pro.

And every guy on every team wants to get into the Super Bowl.

Your football life doesn't get any better than winning the Super Bowl, but being named All-Pro means that you're considered the best at your position in the league. And that means a lot.

At the end of each season, I make up the All-Madden team. All-Madden guys are underdogs who usually don't get much recognition.

I put Brad Benson of the Giants on my team one year because he hadn't been named an All-Pro, but he did a great job blocking the Redskins' Dexter Manley, who *was* All-Pro. If Benson could block an All-Pro, he had to be on *some* team, so I put him on mine.

Being an NFL player doesn't just require physical talent. There's a lot that's in the mind.

Two basic things make up a professional player's attitude. When something good happens to him he doesn't celebrate too long, and when something bad happens, he learns from it if he can, and then forgets it.

I coached a guy named Willie Brown who was such a good cornerback that he's now in the Hall of Fame. He could have a receiver catch a pass on him, but he'd put it right out of his head and have as much confidence as ever.

He'd think, "Okay, you beat me that time, but next time I'm going to make an interception." Willie really believed it.

The eyes of a great defensive player—Hall-of-Fame cornerback Willie Brown.

A guy can drop a pass, and if he's a bad pass receiver he'll keep thinking about the dropped pass. A good receiver thinks, "I'm going to catch the next one."

The same attitude holds for the *good* things that happen. A guy can't catch a touchdown pass and say, "I got it now. I'm going to catch every pass." The next thing you know, he'll be

Chapter 8
Making It
in the NFL
(and Other Ways
to Have a Life
in Football)

thinking about his last catch, and the ball will hit him in the head.

Whatever you *did* is in the past. If you overreact to good or bad things, it's going to affect how you play.

This isn't to say that you shouldn't learn from things. If you're doing something wrong, you have to be able to evaluate it and find out why.

The day after a game, a pro will watch a dropped pass on film and see that he didn't get his hands up, he didn't look it into his hands, he tried to catch it too close to his body and it hit his pads, or whatever caused it. He evaluates his misplay to find out if it was a *technical* mistake, then goes to work to keep that error from happening again.

A pro learns not to get elated when he wins. And he learns not to get too down when he loses. Unless it's the last game of the season, you have to come back and play another game next week.

As a coach, I learned that if I got too happy when we won, I couldn't get started the next day. And when I got down after a loss, I couldn't get started. You have to accept what you did is over. There's nothing you can do about it, win or lose. If you won a big game, the *next* game still starts with a score of 0–0.

Until you've won the Super Bowl, I don't think a team should be celebrating the day after a win. That's the tough thing about life in the NFL. It's tough on the players and on the coaches. No matter what you do one day, you have to come right back the next and start preparing for the next team. And that's what it takes to be part of the pros.

Five Ingredients of Greatness

Four times when I was with the Raiders, I coached the Pro Bowl. That's an honor, but it isn't an honor a coach wants. Coaching the Pro Bowl means you lost the championship game and didn't get into the Super Bowl.

My staff and I figured, since we were there, we might as well learn what made these Pro Bowl players great.

Was it because they're tall? Lean? Stocky? Did they have big arms? We found those weren't the answers. For every tall guy who was great, there was a shorter one just as good. For every speedy guy, there was a slower player just as good.

Finally, we looked for personality traits, and found five qualities each of these players shared.

Toughness

Toughness isn't a macho thing. The great fullback Larry Csonka once defined toughness for me. "Toughness," he said, "is the ability to do everything with the same enthusiasm, including things you don't enjoy."

At the time, Zonk was one of the great first-and-ten players of all time. Everytime he got the ball on first and ten, he'd run it up the middle and people would start piling on his shoulders, his thighs, his legs, his ankles, and finally bring Zonk down. He'd gain eight yards with eleven guys on him.

Nobody enjoys getting hit like that, but it was the job Csonka had to do, and he did it with enthusiasm.

Aggressiveness

Great players win games by making things happen.

I'll never forget a play my Raider cornerback, Willie Brown, made late in 1973. We were playing in Houston, and we were ahead. An Oiler receiver caught a pass across the field, but Willie chased him anyway and hauled him down on the 2-yard line. On the next play, the Oilers fumbled; Phil Villapiano recovered and ran the ball back fifty-two yards. We ended up winning, 17–6, but if Willie hadn't hauled down that receiver, we might have lost.

The really important thing about Willie's play was that he was so far away from the ball, if he hadn't chased the receiver, I wouldn't have noticed. My assistant coaches wouldn't have noticed. But Willie was aggressive, he made something happen. Willie didn't have to chase the receiver, but he did—and caught him.

Pride

Great players have a commitment to be the best and a fear that they might *not* be. That fear of failure motivates them. Without pride, fear of failure is just fear.

In the locker room before a Pro Bowl game, I noticed that O.J. Simpson just couldn't sit still. This wasn't O.J. Simpson the actor and television commercial star. This was the O.J. who had rushed for a record 2,003 yards that season.

I said to him, "Is this game that big to you?"

"Every game is that big," O.J. said. "I don't want to be *one* of the best. I want to be the *best* of the best."

"That's why you are the best of the best," I said.

Knowledge

A player has to not only know how to play his own position, but how all the players on the team play theirs. Any time a tackle says to me, "I'm the tackle, I don't know what the guard does," I'm not impressed. If the tackle doesn't know what the guard does, then he can't really know his *own* job either.

Dedication

Willingness to work. When a great player messes up a play, he'll work until he gets it right. An average player won't. That's why he's average.

Any of these are qualities great players share. How did they get them?

From playing the game.

Index

About the Author

JOHN MADDEN grew up next to his neighborhood's vacant lot in Daly City, California, and was in charge of games at an early age. Later, as head coach for the Oakland Raiders, he became only the second coach in pro football history to win one hundred games during his first ten years. Now, his four Emmy Awards for football analysis and his best-selling books are ample proof that John Madden is America's favorite sports commentator.